Searching Our Souls

(For: Women)

Life–Changing Words Having Relevance to Our Everyday Living – Giving Hope Where There Is None – The 'How To' for the Benefit of Women Desiring to Lead a Happier, Healthier and Prosperous Life Throughout All of Their Relationships.

By

Brenda S. Williams

Author of— 'Searching Our Souls' [For: Men]

© 2002 by Brenda S. Williams. All rights reserved.

No part of this book may be reproduced, stored in a retrieval system, or transmitted by any means, electronic, mechanical, photocopying, recording, or otherwise, without written permission from the author.

ISBN: 1-4033-5280-1 (e-book)
ISBN: 1-4033-5281-X (Paperback)

Library of Congress Control Number: 2002093233

This book is printed on acid free paper.

Printed in the United States of America
Bloomington, IN

1stBooks - rev. 9/20/02

ACKNOWLEDGMENTS:

Acknowledgement of Thanks: Permission Granted for the use of Bible Quotes.

Quotes Taken From: THE HOLY BIBLE–Old and New Testaments in the King James Version

By: Thomas Nelson Publishers–Nashville, Tennessee Copyright Dated 1976

I would like to give my first 'thank you' to my 'Heavenly Father'–GOD, from whom all blessings flow and to my Lord and Savior–Jesus Christ, for my life.

I sincerely 'thank my husband, Melvin, who has been a motivating force in my life. Melvin, you have always been supportive of me through my many endeavors by allowing me the time needed to pursue 'my dreams' and many of those times you had more confidence in me than I had in myself. I love and thank you very much.

A special 'thanks' goes to my daughter, Lisa. Lisa, you have been my sounding board when I was not quite sure of myself, while giving me the inspiration to 'never give-up'. I will always appreciate you, as you have been a blessing to me.

Thanks to my daughter- Maria, my son – Rodney and my three grandchildren – Shayla, Carmen and Quinton (who are the lights of my life) – for loving me unconditionally.

'Thank you' to my most dependable and loving clients, Connie – Beverly – Elizabeth – Charlotte and Louise, who also inspired me to persevere. I love you all and your loyalty has meant a lot to me through the years and I am sincerely grateful.

TABLE OF CONTENTS

PREFACE vii

INTRODUCTION xiii

Chapter One 'THE BEGINNINGS' 1
    Childhood Years...................................... 1
    Approaching Adulthood............................ 2
    Entering Adulthood.................................. 3
    Adult Life.. 3
    Maturity/Spiritual Growth......................... 8
    Respecting Time 10
    Responsibility As An Adult 11

Chapter Two 'LIVING THE SINGLE LIFE' 16
    That 'Special Someone' 17
    Common Ground...................................... 21
    Self Control/Attitude................................ 23
    Good Communication Skills..................... 24
    Misrepresentation..................................... 27
    Take Time To Know Each Other 30
    Being Treated Like 'A Lady' 32
    Past Relationships 32
    A 'Workaholic' 34
    Romance... 35
    Sex vs. Making Love 39

Chapter Three 'LOVE AND MARRIAGE' 45
    Defining 'Love/Loving'............................ 46
    Defining 'Marriage'................................. 48

    Behavior In The Marriage 49
    'Serenity Prayer' 53
    Marital Statistics 55
    Wedding Vows 57
    Admiration and Appreciation 58
    Quality vs. Quantity of Time 62
    Friends 68
    Investing In Your Marriage 73

Chapter Four 'PARENTHOOD' 78
    Becoming A 'Mother' 78
    Discipline and Guidance 81
    'Principles' of Parenting 84
    'Buddy System' 90
    Support of Your Child 91

Chapter Five 'THE SPIRITUAL SIDE OF YOU' 99
    God's Miracle Creation 99
    Our 'Heavenly Father' 101
    Understanding and Forgiveness 105
    Pride/Self Importance 106
    The 'Life of Jesus' 107
    Expectations of Woman 108
    Laws Governing Woman 113

PREFACE

This book is simply composed for ease of reading to assist **woman** in her *search* for happiness and prosperity in all areas of her life. This book does not require you to have a Ph.D., dictionary and/or thesaurus, in order to read it and comprehend what you have read. The only requirements needed are common sense, an open heart and opened mind.

Hopefully this book will mirror into the heart, body, mind and *soul* of those who will pause and take time to read it. Its' purpose is to aid all WOMEN in prospering emotionally, intellectually and spiritually - as well as physically or financially.

As long as you remain human, you will occasionally need to '*search your soul*' for answers that only you can provide - for yourself. Stop for a moment to take a quick overview of your many relationships and yourself, as an individual.

- How well established are your relationships?
- Are your relationships in a harmonious state?
- Are you faced with issues/problems of which you wish - you could simply erase?
- When pressures from issues are presented to you and seem overwhelming, how do you respond to them?
- How do you handle obstacles that appear to block your progress?
- Would you classify yourself as a 'strong woman' or a 'weak woman'?

All of these questions should prompt you to **stop** and '*search your soul*' for valid answers. '*Soul searching*' will supply answers to the whys, whens and hows that are needed to proceed with your life.

As you travel this journey of life, you <u>will</u> continually face problems/issues (from time to time) in your relationships. When they surface, you must be able to handle them! You may be dealing with a problem/issue stemming from your affiliation/union with your spouse, children, relatives, friends and/or associates. These dealings very often create issues that <u>must</u> be addressed without hesitation in order to persevere.

As we all know, relationship means a mutual exchange between two people who have dealings with one another. Our lives do not begin - nor end with the relationship as man and woman but only expand the rapport we will and must come across in this life as we encounter others. Our encounters pose special validity to us in our lives. Some people come to us only passing through, others stay for a limited amount of time, and others will come to remain. In all of these encounters, regardless their length of stay, a relationship is born. Your relationships should form an authentic bond of that which creates a strong foundation to build on. Conscientiously, build on your relationships one-day at a time with reverence [admiration/respect]. This will allow your differences, as they surface, to be handled in an effective manner that will bring understanding.

There are ways of dealing with your problems /issues effectively and it all starts with **You**. Hope, being the confident expectation of filling one's desires, should provide time to handle your problems/issues in a constructive manner. Regardless of the circumstances that created the problems/issues, hope should always be there.

All problems have solutions. Do not become a part of your problems when trying to solve them. This simply means, do not make matters worse, if at all possible. Instead, try to endure the circumstances, providing you know what they are, while bringing a solution (answer) to the problem. Problems do not fix themselves**, people do!** In order to accomplish this, it often means **you** need to make changes in **yourself**. This undertaking allows you to exercise your 'constitutional right' - which is to **choose**. **The greatest of human freedoms is - Choice.** The choices you make in your life will determine your yesterday, today and tomorrow. Carefully make your choices in everything you encounter. If you are in doubt, don't do anything until you are sure of the 'right thing' to do. You must learn how to be discerning [perceptive]. When you are discerning, you will narrow your consequences, eliminate the 'what ifs' and minimize your regrets. Most of all, you will live more of a 'stress-free' life. How well you live your life is completely up to you. Your life belongs solely to '**you**' and the changes '**you**' make within yourself will be based exclusively on your choices that will be ruled by your essence [spirit/basic nature].

In '***Searching Our Souls***', you will find that you have a 'natural power' to make your life what you want it to be as you gain discernment. We all have a certain amount of natural power to make changes to exemplify [demonstrate] the good in our lives. This gives us tremendous control. This control, however, should reign <u>only</u> over your self and not others.

The direction of this book flows towards the majority of WOMEN. [Please Note that I have stated - the <u>majority of women</u>.] If you should be among the few (**if any**) who may have complete order in her life, this book would not apply to you and by all means consider yourself truly 'blessed'- in every way.

In essence, the knowledge provided in this book will enlighten WOMEN, of all backgrounds-race-creed-and color, to a better future in life.

Allow yourself to become one of them!

INTRODUCTION

The standard abbreviation of **S.O.S.** is a Signal of Stress. Although the interpretation of **S.O.S.** may vary to the reader, I have interpreted the abbreviation **S.O.S.** as **'*Searching Our Souls*'.** In '*Searching Our Souls*' you will learn how to stop playing the 'same old roles' and begin a new life for yourself, which will bring you continued peace, happiness and joy.

We live in a very stressful world, which many of us have helped to create. We occasionally allow certain happenings or things to take place in our lives, which often create stressful situations, without being aware of what we are doing. The main reason for this is due to lack of knowledge. If you are not knowledgeable enough to believe in something, you will fall for almost anything. Knowledge, in itself, is power and a very powerful tool: when used appropriately. Knowledge is the tool needed to demonstrate responsibility through all of our many endeavors. In order to have a better understanding of ourselves and learn how to live a less stressful life as adults, knowledge of <u>your</u> <u>self</u> is most important. This is where responsibility begins - **with you**. The time is now for you to take a stronger hold of responsibility in shaping-up [change/correct] your life.

We must try harder to display <u>respect</u> as well as <u>understanding</u> for one another so that men and women will be able to share a good life together. **This is a must**. In doing this justice, you will immediately benefit. The act of respecting and the development of understanding are necessary for healthier living. To make this an easier task, you must engage in "***Searching Our Souls***." In this *search* you <u>will</u> find the understanding that you need to respectfully possess the qualities to live a healthy and happy life.

Although everyone occasionally escapes to a 'fantasy island' of his or her liking, this does not mean to live blindly towards the rest of the world.

Choosing to live your life this way is living a fallacy [an illusion] which is deviation from what is truth. In choosing to live your life this way will create mass confusion. Mass confusion is mainly due to people who choose to be false impressionists [pretender] and not realists. It is important that you understand you are living in a 'real' world and you are a 'real' person. The pretenders of this world, through their fantasies, are merely on stage. There are far too many actresses who have not completed any courses in acting; yet, they want to play a 'starring role'. Are you a mere 'pretender' living in a fantasy world or are you a 'realist', identifying with the fact – **'this world is as real as it gets'**?

Are you an actress on stage and not getting compensated or recognition for your performance? If so, stop and analyze your life situation now. Ask yourself a couple of questions.

- How well is your stage set?

- Are your props (support) in place as they should be so that you feel comfort and secure?
- Are you the Villain or the Heroine in your starring role?
- Who would you rather be?
- Above all, who wrote this play for you?
- (If you cannot provide sound answers to any of the above questions, then obviously you did not write the role you are now playing.)
- <u>Rewrite the script</u>. If you are unhappy in your environment, change your set.
- Create a better prop (support) for yourself. Your environment is very important. It plays a substantial and significant part in your life. After all, your environment is an extension of you.
- Step aside to clearly observe your stage and cast of members. What do you see?
- Do you really have a leading role?

- If so, what role are you staging?

You are only existing when you are lost behind the scenes. You then become trapped in your 'fantasy' world. What will you do? Become the **Heroine** if you've been acting as the Villain. It is a fact; the **Heroine** is a woman of distinguished valor/bravery and <u>always wins</u> admiration: while the <u>Villain,</u> is capable of vile morally hateful deeds and <u>always loses</u>. This, of course, requires you to make some changes. <u>It is never too late to make changes</u>. Make your starring role what it should be, as you '***Search*** your ***Soul***', to gain more peace and happiness as you create a base for security in your life. Although bad habits are sometimes hard to break, changes are not always hard to make. <u>Change takes time</u>. However, through admission of needing to make a change, you will have conquered a valid first step towards living a better life. Continue to bear in mind - '**success will follow effort**'. Nothing changes without your willingness to accept the need of changing. Changes are needed as we continue to live our lives because of adversities [troubles] that we will continually face. You should live your life to its fullest potential and <u>not</u> let life - live you.

It is definitely possible to have a good relationship, if this is what you desire. Begin to make your *search* for genuine happiness and prosper in all areas of your life. Believe [have faith] in yourself and always place your faith and trust in **GOD**. Unlike your fellow man, whom you may have great trust in, **GOD** will never fail you. When we give **GOD** first place in our lives and surrender to "*Searching Our Souls*", we gain discernment [insight] which will guide us to do the things within our hearts that are 'right'.

In the following pages you will understand that you are not alone in your *search*. You will find there are similar, if not the same, problems/issues that many women face. You <u>will</u> and <u>can</u> overcome your problems/issues providing your readiness to take the challenge.

The time to be Ready is **<u>NOW</u>**!

Let's start at the beginning of Chapter 1 of *'Searching Our Souls'* (S.O.S.) to avoid playing the 'same old roles'.

Chapter One

'THE BEGINNINGS'

In the beginning of your life past infancy, life as a child was simple. If not, it should have been. There were responsibilities being handled for you by someone else. This period of time in your life, referred to as your *childhood,* should have allowed you to be free of stress related responsibilities: if any at all. Some of you may have had the responsibility of helping to care for younger siblings, while other children had the 'freedom to <u>simply</u> be a child'. Whatever your *childhood* situation may have been, the bottom line is clear, you didn't have an opportunity to choose for your self. Someone else made the choices for you and those choices were to govern how you were to live your life. Good and bad choices were made, I believe, in all of our childhood days! (How many people do you know who were able to have the childhood of their choice?)

From adolescence to adulthood, your instructions sort of diminished. At this time, you are trusted to demonstrate all that has been taught to you; remembering you have heard the things you should and should not do possibly over and over again. As you are *approaching adulthood*, there are changes experienced through the mind, body, and ***soul***. These changes bring about an awareness of becoming a 'young adult'. Now is the time for you to begin showing more responsibility for yourself. You are looked upon by others to use your better judgment, applying what you have been taught, rather than have someone continue being the judge over you dictating do's and don'ts. In this period of time, you are somewhat understanding what becoming a young woman is partially about. Although you have begun to develop in ways that distinguish you as becoming a 'young woman' oppose to being a child, this is merely a vague beginning to adulthood.

As you are *entering adulthood*, you begin to gain a sense of freedom. You start to feel as though you are at liberty to do as you wish. You have no commitments and no one continuously telling you what you should do or when to do it. Your primary concern is yourself. Would you find this to be conclusively correct? Well, only so much of that is true. However, as you grow in becoming an 'adult', there is a lot of responsibility that should accompany the title. Although you consider yourself an adult, <u>*maturity*</u> **needs** to take place. The only way you will be able to understand what it means to be a 'responsible adult' and gain respect as one is with <u>*maturity*</u>.

You are required, as a 'mature adult', to show <u>complete</u> responsibility for yourself. You now have total control over how you want to live your life. Taking absolute authority of your life ultimately requires you to display responsibility. While being in acceptance of your responsibilities such as: keeping a roof over your head (providing you are on your own), buying your own food, clothes, toiletries etc.; accept the fact that your obligations [responsibilities] have only just begun. Being an 'adult' not only requires income to sustain support for yourself, it also requires that you make important decisions (choices) regarding other areas in your life. Making decisions or choices can often be difficult. Now that you have passed that childhood stage, adolescence, and young adulthood, **your choices are exclusively your own**.

The real challenge is to know when you are making the 'right' decisions/choices. This same challenge was presented to your parents or other persons who assumed responsibility of you when you were a child, and it wasn't any easier for them as it is or will be for you. As an adult, from this point on, your explorations [*search*/discoveries] should be based with this very fact in mind. Adults [fully grown people] hinder their ability to progress when they waste valuable time blaming others for ill wills, which were presented to them in childhood. Grant

Searching Our Souls

you, this is not to minimize what was probably said or done to you when you were a child. This does mean, you can not go through life carrying this type of grief forever. To do this would create a barrier that will only obstruct your forward development. Seek professional help or **let it go and get over it!** You are in charge of yourself and you should not waste time casting blame on anyone else for ill choices that were made prior to this time. After all, why should you? It definitely would not change anything because your past is irretrievable [gone forever]. The only possible way blame could serve you would be <u>only</u> to create a crutch for support or provide you with an excuse to hide behind; should you fail at your own decision-making (choices).

Your choices determine your destiny [future]. (Your future is not years from now; it is - the next moment of today). Take time to gain insight on the direction of your life that leads to your destiny. The outcome of your future is based on the choices/decisions you make today. You should make the best choice possible in order to be content with your self as you proceed through life. <u>Bad choices</u> will certainly predict and produce <u>negative results</u>. Consequently, you will become sad and no doubt - feel bad, sorrowful, or just plain unhappy. <u>Good choices</u> predict and produce <u>positive results</u>. Need I say the effect that positive results will have on you? Making positive choices will help you live a better life, giving you contentment that leads to intense happiness. You have the ultimate power to either feel good or bad. No one else has this power over you, unless you surrender that power. So, when you give that power to someone else to control your 'happiness' and the results does not deliver that of which you were expecting, you have no one to blame but - yourself. Do not give someone else the total responsibility of your life and do not depend on someone else to make you happy and possibly fail at it. You will always be left with a broken heart. Protect your heart and never give all of your heart to anyone unless it is to **JESUS**, for he will never fail you. Take-on the courage to maintain the power you have within and create your own happiness or despair.

'***Searching Our Souls***' will empower you through your inward *search* to obtain discernment [perception/insight] to determine the right choices/decisions while teaching you to be accountable, regardless of the outcome. Acknowledging the 'bad' as well as the 'good' demonstrates *maturity*. The adult woman, who will readily take hold of her responsibilities with the understanding that she is accountable for all that she does, is considered to be a <u>mature adult woman</u>. *Maturity* is vital in making good decisions/choices that will allow you to live your life to its fullest potential, as a WOMAN. Are you there yet? If not, your time has come.

As you travel through this life to reach maturity, have you ever completely hesitated to **'*search* your *soul*'**? If so, what did you find or learn about yourself? Ask yourself this question and be honest with yourself through the deliverance of your answer. **Now that I am a woman, am I the 'best woman' I can be in all areas of my life?** If your truthful answer to this question is **YES**, you should be commended [praised and applauded] because you have not only grown into a <u>mature woman</u> but you have also grown <u>spiritually</u>. This is a great accomplishment and one of which too many others need to proclaim. So many men and women need to gain <u>spiritual</u> <u>growth</u>. Your *search* of happiness is not as hard to find when spiritual growth has taken place. Many women are still in *'search'* of happiness and it is mainly due to the fact of not yet reaching this plateau - spiritual growth. You will become capable of displaying genuine emotion [feeling], when you have attained [achieved] spiritual growth. These feelings will poise [balance] qualities such as kindness, generosity, understanding and above all love. These qualities enable you to demonstrate consciousness by exhibiting tenderness, sensitivity, sympathy, empathy, passion, affection, etc. They are all main ingredients needed to prosper. This prosperity will lead to genuine peace and joy [intense happiness] in all areas of your life. Spiritual growth will define the person you are, without doubt, to - <u>yourself</u>. Meaning, you will be enlightened to your own identity. If you are not at this place in your life, start your *search* within yourself. In your *search* to gain spiritual growth, make use of time wisely. **(Always remember no one lives forever and this includes 'you'.)**

This life that is being given to you is precious. You should respect it by respecting yourself and relish in the joy of being the 'miracle' that you are. **Yes, we are all miracles on this earth**. The 'miracle of life' which sustains [holds/supports] you this day, <u>is truly a blessing</u>. You should utilize each day you are able to awake with a positive attitude towards yourself as well as others. We often waste too much valuable time worrying or planning for tomorrow. When this happens, we rob ourselves of time that we should be spending appreciating the 'given day' in hand. 'Tomorrow' is not promised to anyone and is a part of our future that is unforeseen. 'Yesterday' is irretrievable [gone forever] and is a part of our past that cannot be relived or revised. This is important to remember each day of your life. Learn to live your life, one day at a time.

As we continue to live, the time that will elapse creates a history of our lives. Again, this elapsed time, referred to as our 'past', cannot be retrieved to relive or revise. Live your life <u>today</u> to create a pleasant view of your past; the life that you can be proud of when you reflect back on it in later years to come. Therefore, allow your time to count in a constructive and positive manner. This accomplishment is established through respect. Respecting yourself, others and time are necessary to capitalize [gain/profit] from your life. Learning to *respect time* and using it wisely should be one of your utmost priorities. Time is a valuable asset in all of our lives. Time waits for no one and travels very fast. Don't waste valuable time - especially on unrealistic things. This world is as 'real' as it gets. Don't involve yourself in foolish matters that always have a way of 'haunting you'. This is, for sure, wasted time. The 'present day' is your ultimate concern and based on how well you live this day determines how well you shall live tomorrow. This takes us back to making positive choices by having a positive attitude for yourself and others around you. You should always give thanks to **God** for each day that he gives to you, **which is a 'present'**, because he is giving you another chance to make your life better today than yesterday.

We, who exist on this earth, have a major *responsibility as adults*; regardless of the paths we may choose to walk. We are to be responsible for others as well as ourselves. When and should you encounter someone that stands in the need of help, take hold of responsibility and extend that help to them, if you are able to do so. Reach Out! Being nurtured with love and the understanding of how we are to live our lives taught me how to give of myself.

There is a certain formula we must live by in order to experience joy/happiness in life. That formula consists of placing **JESUS** first in your life, **O**thers second and **Y**ourself third. (Note: the first letters of each will spell – **JOY**.) This is a terminator for selfishness. **It never pays to be a selfish person.** Make use of this formula if there is excessive self-indulgence existing in your life. Give **JESUS** first place because he is the <u>primary</u> reason why you are in existence. Learn how to give more of yourself by reaching out to help others. (You never know when you will be in a position standing in need of the very same help.) Simply by following those two steps, you will <u>always</u> be taken care of by **GOD** - your 'heavenly father'. Living your life based on this formula will open many doors. This is only one example as to how we should be responsible for one another.

If you look around, you will find there are so many things in this world that needs changing or rearranging. These changes are most definitely a part of all of our responsibility. We have in some way contributed to the world's problems, either through deliberate acts or constant blindness of need. When we have the opportunities to extend a helping hand and we choose to walk on by, this is not acting responsibly. The sheer fact stands to remain that there are many people choosing to be recognized as an 'adult' but are not in acceptance of what it takes to be one. If you find areas in need of help and you are able to administer that help, give freely without the asking. Your good deed(s) will not go unnoticed and good will definitely be returned to you. We need to 'clean up our acts' while the opportunity is being given to us. To change your way of thinking will bring about movement. What happened yesterday does not have to happen today. Let's start changing our <u>thinking patterns</u> to extend the Love and caring that is needed to live as **one**.

When you acknowledge problems, '*search* your *soul*' and make the necessary changes in your life to help confirm how much of a <u>woman</u> you really are.

Reality comes to view sooner or later and when problems/issues are facing you, you will feel confident in the manner of which you, the **mature woman,** will handle them.

There are three main factors that will constitute [establish] the statute [measurement] of maturity in a woman and they are:

    1. **Respect for yourself**
    2. **Respect for others**
    3. **Responsibility for all of your actions**

Searching Our Souls

RESERVED FOR SPECIAL NOTES:

Identify yourself and establish a starting point towards a new beginning. [Example: Journal your strengths and weaknesses. This will help you to determine who you are now and where you want to be (as a person) in your life.]

_____
_____
_____
_____
_____
_____
_____
_____
_____
_____
_____
_____
_____
_____
_____

Chapter Two

'LIVING THE SINGLE LIFE'

How are you choosing to live your life? Are you a single woman living the so-called *'single life'*? If so, have you found fulfillment? Are you completely satisfied or only content with being 'single'? Are you single because you have not found that 'special someone' to share the rest of your life with? Or, could it possibly be that you are single because **it is your divine choice**? There are different types of men and women in the universe. There are some people who desire 'marriage', while others want to remain 'single'. Therefore, whatever desire one has to live his life, the choice is completely up to the individual.

Many women have stated, through my personal survey, their concerns regarding the possibilities of finding the right person or *'**soul** mate'* to share their lives with. This is a serious concern for the 'single woman' that <u>does</u> <u>not</u> want to remain 'single' for the rest of her life. You see these types of women are not afraid of commitment [bonding in agreement] and they have grown to the point of understanding themselves. They feel the need for true [legitimate] companionship. They have a desire to share life's experiences with a committed someone. Are you this type of woman? I am a true believer in there being someone for everyone, as I am a true believer that men and women were created to unite in a bonding agreement such as, 'matrimony'. Providing you have a similar theory of life, are you still ***searching*** *for that 'special someone'?*

Let's take a look at some of the questions on main issues women seem most concerned with, while playing the so-called field, in search of that *'special someone'*.

Some of their concerns are:

- Will the man I meet become my significant other one-day?

- Am I the woman who he has been in *search* of?
- Is he in *search* of a good time or is he in *search* of a lasting relationship?
- Can I be what he really needs and wants?
- Is he really the man he seems to be or the man I see him as being?
- Will he become the father of my children someday?
- The list goes on. Answers to all of these questions will be acknowledged in time. Take your relationships, **one day at a time**. The fact here is - time will tell. Believe me, time has a way of telling it all.

Let's view some of the possibilities and probabilities of life while in *search* of that '*special someone*'. If you consider yourself as being 'normal', you should be in *search* for a 'normal' man. [Normal meaning emotionally sound/well-adjusted.] This type of man will probably add much happiness to your life providing you are 'normal' and equally committed to each other. Well-adjusted men and women have normal needs and desires often leading to marriage. They have hopes and share dreams of building a life together. Since the beginning of time, this has always been considered the "norm". There are women who do not want a committed relationship and are not considering ever to be married. Of course, this is what they will tell you. Although, this does not signify that these types of women are not normal, there is an underlying reason as to why they are not able to find someone they can commit to. Maybe they are **searching** in the wrong places for that *'special someone'* or simply need to change their approach. Whatever the reasons are, as to why they cannot find who they are possibly looking for, they will readily provide some excuse [justification] trying to substantiate why they are still - alone. Could this be a fair assessment of you and your ways? Have you ever found yourself trying to defend why you are not in a committed relationship? First of all, you must be completely realistic/sensible in your **search,** if you are looking for your – 'Mr. Right'. <u>Acknowledge the fact</u> - there are no 'perfect men' residing in this world. The sooner you accept this fact, the easier your quest will be and your **search** will not seem as though it is eternal [never-ending]. Looking for a man to be that of which you have fantasized about and complied into one 'great big package', is not in existence. However, a 'good man' is not hard to find and there are many of them on this earth. (**YES**, they have their faults too.) If you are a 'good woman' (despite of your faults and imperfections) and position yourself in ways that will reflect your 'good' character [spirit], your man will be able to find you! <u>Obtain</u> and <u>maintain</u> respect for yourself and you will – hopefully one day - attract someone who will have respect for you as well as themselves.

Remember everyone has faults /imperfections. Therefore, while you pursue your journey seeking

'Mr.Right' and expecting him to have zero flaws, you will never end your *search*!

Various women are not willing or simply cannot live with the companionship of another person on a permanent basis, such as marriage. If this is you, that's okay also. That is your choice. After all, there are men in this world who share the same feelings. As a single person and after time, you become possessive of your space while growing a little bit selfish and cannot compromise in a union – such as marriage. Should you feel this way, staying 'single' is probably your 'best bet'.

I have found there is much <u>common ground</u> women share. Most men do not seem to identify with the need of addressing problems/issues on an intimate level when they arise, **as if the problems/issues will take care of themselves**. This is very annoying to most women. Men are sometimes too evasive when it comes to confronting issues and even more so if they are 'guilty'. They just would rather not discuss things at all and that can insinuate a 'lack of importance'. This definitely does not help any situation. Unfortunately, your problems/issues <u>will not</u> disappear or be erased without attention. It just doesn't work that way. One thing is certain; your problems/issues must be dealt with and not over looked as though they do not exist. This is a <u>must,</u> in order that you move on with your life. Your problems/issues have a way of haunting you when they are left unresolved. All of the above applies to 'men' as well as 'women'. After all, the relationship you are in includes the two of you. If you have been avoiding issues, humble yourself to understand where the origin [root/source] of the problem lies. This is your starting point. For it may be YOU.

It is understandable when a woman becomes perturbed when her man cannot effectively deal with their problems/issues and takes the 'macho' approach. Some men will readily become 'the self-proclaimed [appointed] macho man' to try and prove their point, while losing sight of the real problem

/issues at hand. This behavior does not, nor will it ever, solve your problems/issues. It does not prove anything other than a lack of *self-control* [discipline]. It only complicates things and actually makes them worse. Women often are guilty of this same aggressive behavior when they are approached. Learn to substitute aggressiveness – which is being hostile - with tact. [Tact always demonstrates an understanding of how to avoid offending.] Avoid putting someone on defense while trying to get your message across. You will only 'shut down' the other person when you behave in this manner. What you have to say will not have any meaning because you will not be heard. You must <u>exercise *self-control*</u> [self-discipline] in order to allow time for understanding, while getting to the root of the problem. Attitude is very significant in all that you do. Attitude plays a great part in problem solving. Your disposition [attitude] is important because that which you translate to others is exactly what you will receive. If you approach someone in a calm manner, they will reciprocate. [They are willing to be more giving and will listen to you.] When you direct anger towards someone, they will retaliate. [They will return blow for blow or seek revenge.] Again, being aggressive immediately puts one on defense and your voice will not be heard. **This is a lesson that is worthy of being <u>learned</u>**. This will enable you to 'think' before you 'speak'. Once you have conquered *self-control*, you will always be able to solve your problems effectively through better communication skills.

Good communication skills are very important in all areas of our lives. Good communication is the foundation in <u>any</u> relationship. It has most often been referred to as a 'life line'. Learn how to effectively communicate with people in your life. If you are curious about something, don't be afraid to <u>ask questions</u>. When given an answer, <u>listen closely</u> and <u>pay strict attention</u> to what is actually being said. It is not safe to assume things about another person, especially if you are able to ask them questions and they are able to answer. Don't become offended if <u>you</u> are asked questions. Try to answer questions asked of you as honestly as you can. Most people are not 'mind readers' and should not be expected to become one. So often we expect the other person to know what we are thinking and feeling. This places a great responsibility on the other person. Also, this is very unfair to do. Relieve the people in your life of such major responsibility and learn how to tell them what you are thinking and feeling, especially when asked. They in return, should be able to do the same thing in respect of you. Keep the doors to good communication opened. When we are able to talk **<u>to</u>** one another and not **<u>at</u>** one another, our voices will be heard. This helps you to create a level of more complete understanding. I can not express enough importance on <u>*good communication*</u>. This is a **'golden key'** that can unlock many doors. So often people are misunderstood because of the lack of good communication. When good communication is absent, you close the doors to your ***soul*** and therefore your relationships become doomed for failure. Know the importance of *good communication skills* and learn to master them. Making positive comments always out weight negative ones. Teach yourself to be a positive thinker. This will produce a positive demeanor [behavior] that will be displayed in all areas of your life.

While playing the field, you will one day find the person that seems to be compatible with you. When you find that person, honesty is very important and <u>will</u> determine the longevity of your relationship. Honesty should be in place whether you are contemplating marriage or not. The outcome of your relationships will never last when you are untrue to yourself. You see; the main relationship that should be in order is with - **yourself**. Regardless of whom you choose to spend time with in your life, the life you are living starts with '**you**'. Be proud of who '**you**' are. If you can't be proud of yourself, <u>**you**</u> need to make some changes. This is easy to do if you

Searching Our Souls

are not 'performing' [trying to cover up the 'real you'/ pretending to be someone that you're not]. If you have been living your life as 'The Pretender', you have a lot of work to do in changing yourself. In living this way, you have deceived yourself and all others around you. This is referred to as misrepresentation.

Men have expressed *misrepresentation* [deceit] to be a major problem they face as their relationship grows. Most men feel women play a great game of '*misrepresentation*'. Some men have dated women to find they are not at all, who or what they claim to be. After awhile, the real deal comes to view. [Meaning the real – **YOU.**] When these types of women are confronted, they often cannot bear proof nor have they ever 'practiced' what they may be 'preaching'. This is the results of false impressions and in time, will bring many problems into any relationship. **Stop misrepresenting yourselves! This is exactly what is happening when you try to be something or someone that you're not.** You hurt yourself in the long run, as well as others, through the betrayal of honesty. When this happens, it is very hard to regain the same trust of someone. As you go along, painting an untrue image of yourself, you had better walk carefully. The 'real' you will definitely surface - one day. Proof of this fact has been established and confirmed by the old expression that says, "you can run, but you sure can't hide". Play it safe and <u>deliver yourself as you are</u> and allow people to have the choice to 'like' or 'dislike' you. It becomes really tiring to keep up the role as 'a pretender' and far less stressful to be 'real' [honest/true]. **A lie will always need altering but the "truth" never needs changing, <u>for it remains the same</u>.** Let this be of help to you, if you have been living your life as a 'lie'. Reach within to '*Search* your *Soul*' and come to terms with the 'real' you that you have been defrauding [cheating on] and concealing [hiding/masking]. Procure [obtain] the understanding that jewelry, clothes and/or make-up does not spell 'who' you are, nor does it tell all of 'what' you are about. I am quite aware, as many others, that conceitedness has taken over the minds of many women and they can't get past trying to 'look good' on the <u>outside</u> long enough to ever consider that their focus should be to 'look good' inside - **first**. (The last time I checked, **beauty** <u>was</u> still found – <u>skin deep</u>!) Please ladies, dress from the inside – out! Your appearance will take on a 'look' it never has before. You will become beautiful in 'spirit' and therefore your complete essence will be one that is 'attractive' to all. If you are a woman looking for a 'real' man, may I suggest you become a 'real' woman! Get to know yourself. You should take time to know yourself better as an individual, in order to build a relationship with another individual. Making the necessary alterations in <u>your</u> <u>own</u> <u>life</u> will give you the freedom to be 'who' you really are with confidence in your relationships and you will find being 'honest' is not hard at all. You may find being 'honest' as quite comforting. Comforting to the point of really <u>knowing</u> 'who' you are and never having to 'lie' in order to be accepted.

Now that you know yourself better, *take time to get to know that someone you've just met.* You should always 'take time' in getting involved in your relationships. Again, I cannot emphasize this enough. This is where so many men and women seem to make their greatest mistake. Time is needed in your relationship to gain more of a complete understanding of the other person. This opportunity is not always fairly extended. When things go wrong, people will so readily speak negatively on the character referencing the other person. This is not possible when you are not thoroughly acquainted with someone. Yet, if the relationship ends, the most injured partner will describe the character of the other partner in disapproving ways (which often defames their character). This is so undignified. While a person goes around tarnishing someone's image, they have not hesitated to consider what they are saying about themselves. It takes a great deal of time to learn the 'good' and the 'bad' in anyone. Allow yourself to become like a <u>sponge</u> and <u>soak up</u> all that is of 'great importance' about the person you are becoming familiar with. When you learn as much as possible about the other person and they learn as much as possible about you, your relationship will stand a better chance of survival. **It is a known fact, <u>rushing-in</u> can and will surely cause you to <u>rush-out.</u>** <u>Good character</u> should be the '*ultimate possession*' in yourself as well as anyone you may be in *search* of. Good character in a person will exhibit morals and values that are established in their life. Morals and values are assets to the beholder - as well as anyone who should encounter the beholder. As time goes on, all of a person's <u>assets</u> [strengths] as well as <u>liabilities</u> [weaknesses] will be revealed. *Take your time*. Always remember there is 'good' and 'bad' in everyone. **No one is perfect**. Therefore, everyone is entitled to be given the **<u>'opportunity of chance'</u>**.

Another main issue women spoke on regarding problems/issues in their relationships revolves around <u>not</u> being '*treated like a lady*'. It seems as though most men have forgotten **chivalry**. <u>**Chivalry means an honorable behavior especially towards women: being respectful – courteous**</u>. The man who identifies with chivalry always behaves as a 'gentleman'. You, as a woman, should want to see this quality in your man. You should want to be treated with **respect** and **courtesy**. The man who is capable of chivalry, without a doubt, possesses charm and that charisma is a quality a woman can forever admire. You see, when a man sees you as a '*lady*' and you are maintaining respect for yourself, he has no other choice than to treat you 'like a lady'; that is - if he's a 'real man'. If you have chosen a man to spend <u>quality time</u> with, he should always <u>***'treat you like a lady'.***</u>

Some men stated their female friends would constantly talk about *past relationships*. Don't bring your *past relationships* into your present relationship. Let your past either be a stumbling block or a learning tool, <u>only to yourself</u>. A man does not always appreciate hearing episodes relating to you and some other man, especially if you have not been asked. {Understand, he may not be interested in where you may have been or what you may have had, but only where you are planning to go and what you have to offer at the present time.} Things of this nature will cause a man to feel as though he is being compared to another man. Any man, in his sound mind, would not appreciate being compared to another man; and any woman, in her sound mind, would not make the comparison known to him. Who you choose to think of and/or compare, when you are alone, is your business. However, your man wants to know that he is the only one on your mind when you are with him, just as you would appreciate this like behavior. If you are living in your 'past' with someone else constantly on your mind and making obvious comparisons of that person, you will soon become a part of your current mates 'past'. Be consciously aware when taking part in conversations regarding your *past relationships*. Your primary concern should be how well your relationship evolves [progresses] with your present mate and not how well you've evolved [progressed] with others. **Keep the scores from your track record to yourself!**

Men also spoke on problems referencing their mates work. Some men stated their mate/companion would constantly talk about work. Too much time is wasted in this manner and does not always benefit one to constantly discuss their job-related problems. Have you ever been classified as being this type of person? If so, this says you do not know how to separate yourself from your work mentally although you are not there physically. This describes a man or woman as a '*workaholic*'. When this happens, you are not being attentive to your mate. This is an infringement [invasion] on time you should be spending when you're together. This, definitely, is not good. Although the job may provide the income to pay the bills, all work and no play can make you a very dull person. If this sounds familiar to you, gain control over your work vs. your other meaningful areas of life, such as time spent with your loved one(s). You are in desperate need of what is referred to as 'balance'. If you need to bring your job [work] into your relationship provide equally as much time to the relationship making it <u>work</u> for you. Believe me, you can not be in two places at the same time. Although you are a miracle creation, there is no way you can be that flexible. When you leave work, remain separated mentally from it until the time comes for you to report, physically. There is a time and a place for everything. If you can relate to that, be conscious of yourself and try to leave work where it belongs, **<u>at work</u>**. Should your work/business exist solely at home, schedule your working hours and stick to them. Utilize the balance of hours in your day on other matters/concerns.

Another issue most women were affected by entailed *romance*. It seems as though men are not as romantic as they could be because they generally expect the woman to handle that department. *Romance* is merely affectionate love that we, as humans, need to give more of - to each other. There are several ways to display affection and it does not always start in the 'bedroom'. In view of the following simple forms to show affection, you will find that you, nor your man, will need to be a 'rocket scientist' or a 'millionaire' in order to be 'romantic'. Here are just a few of them. To plan an evening out to a romantic dinner or dancing is not the sole responsibility of the woman. Your man should take the equivalent of time to make plans for a 'romantic evening' also. I am sure you can sometimes appreciate having the choice to make, but to have an evening planned without your help, would probably mean more to you and make you feel 'very special'. This is a small gesture that most women know how to appreciate and will readily accept from her man. If your man does not do this for you, make the suggestion known to him. Convey your feelings on the matter of sharing a romantic evening together. (If he took the time to 'wine' and 'dine' with you prior to - getting you, let him know he needs to continue - in order to keep you!) *Romance* is not specifically designed to please women. Men benefit great pleasures from romance as well. You, as the woman, should reach out to your man and do something nice for him. Other ways of showing your affectionate side to your mate/partner can simply be accomplished through buying candy, flowers, or cologne. You can always make a quick trip to the card shop. (None of these items are expensive! As I stated to the men: should your income allow you to make purchases on a more upscale level, go for it!) Women appreciate the idea of receiving flowers, candy, perfume, cologne or greeting cards and so do men. Men are not exiled [outlawed] from receiving these gifts. These gifts are more appreciated if there is <u>no</u> 'special occasion' for them to be given. Flowers are not a 'feminine' gift! <u>Men are not partial to flowers</u>. When a person dies, man or woman, flowers are always given to the 'deceased'. Why not give flowers to your man while he is still living? A bouquet of flowers has a way of spelling love to him - <u>your love</u>. Greeting cards are always there to express what you can't always verbalize [speak] from your heart. Make a one-stop trip to the nearest department store and buy him soaps or cologne that smells good to you that you would like to smell more often - on him. Another sure-fire magnet to your loved one's heart is a 'good meal'. All men love 'good food' and especially when time has been taken to prepare it for him. This always spells caring. These of course, are ways to let your man know that he is in your thoughts and he will also acknowledge the sensitivity in you, as his woman. I am sure that many of you enjoy candy, cologne, and greeting cards; and let's not forget that a flower can help to decorate any one's home. As you give some of those perks [rewards], in time some of those perks should be returned to you. **Just as you aim to please - <u>you</u> should be pleased!**

Searching Our Souls

If you are only in *search* of a good time, you should make this clear. Communicate this to your partner/mate. While you're not allowing yourself to become serious minded to develop a lasting relationship, the other person sharing your life deserves to know this. If you want no commitments, say so! Speak openly on where you want or don't want your relationship to travel. With this type of understanding, no one will be hurt. Exercise your mind to determine what you want out of the relationship and convey your thoughts to your partner. As time goes by, we begin to develop 'feelings' that we often refuse to identify with. This is mainly due to the fact of simply not knowing exactly what it is that we are 'feeling'. We ask ourselves, "Is this *love or lust* that I am feeling?" Yet, those feelings often influence us to take our relationship to a higher level, the level of intimacy [emotional closeness]. Many will go forth following their feelings, taking part in intimate relations [intercourse] and fail to consider the consequences that could result from their actions. You see, when you engage in intercourse, this is a 'sexual union' that should have special meanings to both of you. Although this union is a form of communicating, this interchange should <u>only</u> display genuine Love. Sexual encounter should only take place when two people are absolutely in love. Understand love is not only what you <u>feel</u> for a person, it is also what you <u>do</u> for a person. When you experience a sexual act with someone, it often heightens your boundaries in the relationship. Love becomes prevalent [common/accepted] to one or both people engaging in sex. This is how it should be. You should also realize that feelings change and those feelings can interpret words without them being said. So, what are you telling your partner/mate? Are you telling him that you really 'care' and feel 'genuine love' for him or are you viewing him as another 'conquest'? *Are you making 'love'* or merely having *'sex'* – 'casual sex'?

Searching Our Souls

In today's world, there are too many people, young and old, who engage in 'casual sex'. There is strong <u>lack</u> of self-control in this area. Sadly enough, 'love' does not come in to play. There are major distinctions in *'making love'* oppose to *'having sex'*. If you are in lust and not caring with your heart, you are not *making 'love'* - you are merely *having sex*. When you are in lust, you are not genuinely caring. The only thing that you are getting is a temporary 'quick' thrill. Let's face it! *'Making love'* takes a great deal longer and is by far more satisfying than a temporary 'quick' thrill. Seek to find love - first - from your heart. The heart is the place where 'love' originates. If you are only in lust, whereas sex is the only thing you're thinking of and he means only another conquest to you, you should think again about your intentions. Your actions are based only on impulses, due to raging hormones and you are only using someone to satisfy a biological need. When you do this, you are taking advantage of not only their body but their heart as well. This behavior more simply stated is '**using**'. If you are only 'using' him, this is wrong. Do not use any man only to satisfy your sexual-biological need. How would you like it if you were to find out that you were simply being 'used'? Don't <u>use</u> anyone for any reason as far as that is concerned. This behavior spells deceit. Deceitfulness will only make <u>you</u> the 'fool' when the truth comes to view. Therefore, 'always treat other people as you would like to be treated'. There is no doubt in that statement. It plainly means just what it says. What goes around surely comes around and the things you do, can and will surely, come back to you. (This means whether they are good or bad.) If your actions are not based with this thought in mind and you are deceiving someone, there will be many hurt feelings to come as a result. Stop to consider someone else and their feelings and put yourself in their place. Again, apply the thought of 'how you would like to be treated'.

Through experience, try mastering the art of love – genuine love. It has many rewards. Remember that

Searching Our Souls

experience is meaningless if you do not learn from it.

RESERVED FOR SPECIAL NOTES:

From this chapter, list your identifying (related) problems/issues and give 'no restraint' to what you may have found within yourself as a 'reality'.

_____
_____
_____
_____
_____
_____
_____
_____
_____
_____
_____
_____
_____
_____
_____
_____

Chapter Three

'LOVE AND MARRIAGE'

Love – Love – Love - how often we repeat this word. Some people use this word repeatedly and have not an inkling as to what it really means when they use it.

<u>What's your definition of *Love*</u>? *Love* is defined, in my dictionary, as a powerful emotion that is displayed and felt for another person, which manifest itself in the heart and ***soul***. That is such a pleasant and admirable definition given to a word which has, unfortunately, been used out of context on such a regular basis. We speak the word and sometimes fall short in displaying it's meaning. We should remain mindful of the manifestations that powerful emotion brings which are patience, understanding, tenderness and trust. It is a necessity for people to understand that ***love*** is a wonderful gift

and we should extend this gift to each other with benevolence [loving kindness/good will]. *Love* deserves respect and you should learn to give it respect. *Love* is a 'treasure' that matters in all of our lives.

There is no greater feeling in life when you know that you are loved. The feeling is even greater, when you know you are capable of giving love in return. [*Loving* is an art, the action of which love is displayed.] *Loving* gives us as humans, empowering strength to encounter almost anything. *Love* is like a vitamin to heal the **Soul**. Love has the capability to provide us with incredible strength to face the cares and concerns of each passing day. To *Love* and be *Loved* are two of the greatest joys of life. You should first learn to *love* yourself. Although it's not <u>all</u> about you, it starts with you. If you *love* yourself, you will know how to *love* someone else. When you take part in *loving* someone, you not only open the door to your heart - the door to their heart opens as well. You are placing yourself, as well as the other person, in a vulnerable position. When you become vulnerable, you are then capable of being hurt or wounded because there is insufficient protection of your heart. However, you should not allow this to stand in the way of receiving the *love* someone is trying to give to you and by all means-do not hold back from giving the *love* you have within.

As feelings grow and become stronger, you begin to deal with affairs of the 'heart' on a different level. As we know, the heart is a muscular organ. Its main function is to force the blood through the circulatory system. The heart is the vital point of our being. The heart is also the source or fountain of man's deepest feelings such as love, kindness, empathy, sympathy, affection, etc. All of mans' emotions are stored within his heart. In '***Searching Our Souls***', you will become in tuned to all of these elements and when those of which you feel in your heart are sincere, you will begin to identify with them on a more relevant basis - as you continue to live. From *love* emerges affection, which leads to desires that display fondness, devotion and passion. With *love* being such a powerful emotion one feels for another, you should not toy with ones' emotions. You and your partner should be on the same level of understanding especially when it comes to - *love*. If and when you find that you are in love and want to share the rest of your life in marriage with that special someone, *loving* should feel 'natural' and not 'demanding'. You cannot force this feeling on anyone else and you should not want to. You cannot demand *love* from someone simply because you find that you are 'in *love*' with them. If the feeling should be mutual [balanced/equivalent], you will be destined to become one. This destiny results in a union referred to as '**matrimony**'.

Matrimony [*Marriage*] is a union [partnership], under which two people become legally united on a permanent basis and are willing to compromise [give and take] – sacrificing [forfeiting] only their selfishness, should it exist. *Marriage* is not an easy endeavor [venture]. *Marriage* is most definitely a

Searching Our Souls

full-time job and its' success depends on the degree of commitment from the two people involved. There is hard work in making a *marriage* 'successful'. You are two different human beings sharing a life together. It is most important that women (and men) understand themselves and each other in order to live in matrimony.

Men are very much indifferent [somewhat detached and often unemotional] than women. Men are looked upon to be the guide [leader] and guard [protector] as well as provider [supplier] in his marriage. He is to be the 'head of the household' and is driven by facts [actuality - that which is visible to him] more readily than women. Women, however, are 'nurturers' [caretakers] to their husbands and child/children and are driven by sensibility [sensitivity/emotion]. These differences will exist in men and women as long as 'earth-is-earth'.

It is unfortunate that men will often exhibit an ill [unfavorable] emotion [*behavior*] when trying to solve their problems. A vast majority of women have validated this to be true and have concluded the fact, that many men share the same characteristic flaws. One major character flaw in most men, that is responsible for things getting out of hand, is 'voice inflection' [a change of tone or pitch of voice.] Women have experienced this as a major problem in their marriage. Men can not understand the unpleasant impact this has on a woman. Men will take on this type of an approach and things rapidly go down hill. What's being solved by this *behavior*? **Nothing!** Convey to your husband how his tone reflects an image of aggressiveness and let him know how it makes you feel - if you are dealing with this as an issue. Until you voice your feelings, you will probably continue to view this as a problem: one of which could be avoided if you 'speak up'. Women are often guilty of the same *behavior* when trying to communicate with their husbands. When you, as the woman, speak to your husband in this manner he undoubtedly will feel the same as you. [Example: When your husband raises his voice to be heard, this often signifies that he is yelling or disciplining you as though you were not an adult. When you raise your voice to be heard, he feels the same.] Have you not ever told your husband that, "he was not your Father" or he has told you that, "you are not his Mother"? You married your husband to be your 'husband' and not a 'father' to you. He also married you to be his 'wife' and not his 'mother'. You can say anything nicely and it will be accepted – but when you speak loudly or harshly, you have just compounded your problems/issues. This should definitely be avoided in order to keep 'peace' in your marriage. Regardless of the uniqueness of species, you should remember to treat each other in a 'loving manner'. Again, *love* is not only what you 'feel' for another, it is also what you 'do' towards one another.

You can learn from each other as long as you accept the other person for 'who' they are and not try to change them into being who **you** want them to be. This seems to be the hardest of all for many people to understand (especially married people). An example of this: When issues/problems are confronted and your views on the subject matter vary [differ], accept the fact that your spouse is capable of having his own opinion and his opinion does not necessarily need to be identical or mesh with yours. This demonstrates the uniqueness in species and in your personalities. Your man should appreciate the fact of your having a mind of your own and he should allow you to use it. You cannot always agree on everything. It can not always be 'your' way or 'no' way at all.

We often allow our different views to constitute [create/develop] a debate. If you will view your difference of opinion as a simple 'difference of opinion', you will find there is nothing (the majority of the time) to argue about. When you try to force another person to 'think' the same way you are thinking, you are trying to change that person. You have a mind of your own and so do they. The sooner you <u>accept</u> this fact, the better off - **you will be**.

Searching Our Souls

Trying to change another person is a major challenge and one in which <u>you will not</u> succeed.

How aware are you of the ***'Serenity Prayer'***? For the benefit of those who are not familiar with the ***'Serenity Prayer'***, it is as follows:

<u>'SERENITY PRAYER'</u>

Please GOD, grant me:

The <u>SERENITY</u> to accept the things I cannot change,

The <u>COURAGE</u> to change the things I can, and

The <u>WISDOM</u> to know the difference.

<u>Serenity</u> means the quality of being at peace with ones self. **<u>Courage</u>** is the quality of being brave. **<u>Wisdom</u>** is the quality of being wise to know. Adopt this prayer for guidance in your everyday living. By all means, let your mind absorb this prayer to use as a <u>daily guide</u> through your life. Also remember; change needs to take place in all of us as

we continue to grow. However, concentrate on making changes within yourself - only. A person, first, has to acknowledge the areas of his life that needs changing. No one can or should assume this task - other than the individual. Until a person realizes he or she needs to change **self,** change will not take place. Changing most surely displays **serenity** in your self and it takes great **courage** to have the **wisdom** to do so.

Allowing **God** to exist in your life and utilizing the above prayer, on a daily basis, will provide you with each of those qualities to become a better person - enabling you to live a less stressful and uncomplicated life. You will also learn how to love unconditionally and learn how to be very giving at heart. To love unconditionally is to love without expecting an immediate reward and to love without having someone meet your qualifications [needs/requirements]. This is known as 'giving'. Your heart opens and this empowers you to commit [trust]. Give the best of **you** to your spouse and your spouse should do likewise unto you. In doing this, you **will not** become a statistic or end-up in 'an arrangement' - opposed to a '*marriage*'.

Statistics have shown 50% of marriages end in divorce. Why? Some people can not compromise or do not know how to make sacrifices for one another and constantly go about their way trying to transform [change] each other. These types of people are very selfish and they have not lived their lives with the '***Serenity Prayer***' to guide them in their marriage. If you do not know how to <u>sacrifice</u> and you are not willing to <u>compromise</u>, then marriage is not for you. For these are two acts of humanity you must possess and maintain when <u>entering</u> into a union such as '**matrimony**' and <u>remain</u> in that union.

Of the 50% of marriages that end in divorce, some have re-entered the union with hopes of making it last the 'second time around'. This is possible if they are able to identify with the problems that were created in their *marriage* the 'first time around'. **Note:** If you were the problem and failed to come to terms with that very fact, you will (without a doubt) still be the problem existing in your second marriage. To reiterate, it does not matter how many times you choose to marry, your marriage will not be successful because if you were the problem in the first marriage, **without change**, **You** are <u>still</u> the problem.

60% of Marriages, the second time around, end in divorce because they never learned the above. One would think marriage would be better the second time around but unfortunately, this is not necessarily true. Again, the same person divorced in the first marriage will be the same person divorced in the second marriage and so on. Therefore, change what needs <u>changing in you</u>, to give your marriage the chance of survival. (This change is needed in all of your relationships, and not just your marriage.) Should you end up in a divorce, make sure it was not '**you**', as the major <u>problem</u> existing in your

Searching Our Souls

marriage. **Try to identify with ways of making changes in yourself to become a better person.**

In marriage, you are traveling on a street that goes both ways. It takes two. It is no longer all about you. You have not only yourself to consider but your spouse as well. Always remember the *vows* you both took on your wedding day. They <u>usually</u> include '<u>for better or worse</u>' and '<u>till death do us part</u>'. I feel there are too many men and women who do not take their vows seriously. They are not just conjugated [combined/united], structured words that you should say to one another that have no meaning. **They have very specific meanings.** Those *vows* were presented to you to repeat to each other because they are words that you will need to <u>remember</u> and <u>rely</u> on in order to endure [survive] and sustain [support] your marriage. Remember and rely on them whenever necessary, such as troubled times, throughout your marriage. You will find your vows to be very helpful as you build your years together. Other vows included, '<u>to love-honor-and obey</u>'. These are most important ones. <u>Love</u>, should be the main reason as to why you joined in 'matrimony', in the first place. Secondly, with true love, there should always be respect, which is <u>honor</u>. Last but not least, the most misunderstood word – <u>obey</u>. This word merely means to be submissive to each other (within reason) and above all else, the two of you should <u>obey</u> **GOD** in order that you have a fruitful life together. There has been a lot of controversy regarding the word 'obey' in marriage vows. Often people have chosen not to include this word in their vows because they did not understand it's meaning entirely. It is not meant that you should obey as in, doing <u>everything</u> your husband tells you and vise-versa, but it most surely means that the two of you should be obedient to <u>**GOD**</u>. It is because of <u>his</u> 'Amazing Grace' that enabled your 'two' hearts to become filled with **love** to stand before each other having the desire to become 'one'.

Now that you have become one, show your *<u>admiration</u>* and *<u>appreciation</u>* for your spouse and he

Searching Our Souls

should do likewise unto you. Learn ways of showing *admiration* for your husband's many efforts as well as your *appreciation*. This is a valid way of displaying your **love** for him. He needs to know that you appreciate him. He is your husband showing through his many ways that he cares about you as well as himself. (Hopefully this is your husband's character.) Just as you need love (his love) as fuel to keep on going – so does he need love (your love). Your kind words or small gestures of love give him the strength to face another day. When you have a good man by your side as your husband, lover and as a friend, you should start today taking time out to '**Thank God**' for the blessings that he has granted unto you and don't take your husband for granted.

If your husband is the kind of man who is a good father to your child/children, a good provider, respects you as a person, a lover and can take time out to be your friend; be extremely grateful. (For here, you are truly blessed.) Very few women share the same treasures. Some men do not possess all of what is needed to be a good husband to his wife and/or a good father to his child/children. (As some women do not always possess those qualities either and are not completely deserving of someone who does.). A *good woman* will readily assume her responsibilities in the capacity of her life. You as a wife, mother, lover and friend deserve respect and admiration as well as appreciation for respectfully assuming your responsibilities. It has always seemed as though women wear many hats and usually find themselves having to be 'Super Woman' trying to fulfill that which is expected of her. As she takes on these many responsibilities and tries to maintain mostly everything in her life, from anything that should exist between her and her man/family, this alone can become overwhelming. Your husband should recognize this. When you feel your many efforts are not being recognized or appreciated, frustration takes place. Don't allow yourself to become over powered with your responsibilities. You must learn to prioritize. Separate that which is of more importance from that of lessor importance. Take care of the most important things first and later move on to the rest. Ask your husband for assistance if you need it. Don't worry about what he thinks or feels regarding your asking for his help. Try asking and not complaining. If a woman has to complain in order to receive help, most men readily say that she is 'nagging' or that she is 'hard to satisfy'. For most women, this is most untrue and undeserving. A woman who is REAL [sincerely/truly committed to her marriage] and is giving her all and hardly ever receives help from her husband - has every right to 'complain'. After all, most of the things you do should be to benefit you both. With assistance from your husband, you will not become overwhelmed and this alone will enable you to be a more pleasant person to him and your child/children as well as others around you. Learn how to balance your responsibilities in order to maintain a pleasing demeanor [attitude].

If you are a working woman, you are entitled to come home from your hard day at work, tired and drained, just as your husband. Your outside job responsibilities may have ended but when you enter into your home environment, your responsibilities begin, again. Again being a wife, a mother, a friend, a lover, in addition to a 'bread winner' (just to name a few), is a very hard job that has no end and is often **understated** in its entire importance. By all means, you need your husband's help and it should be given without the asking. He should learn how to be more observant as well as understanding of your many responsibilities. When you take time-out to be there for 'him', he should take time-out to be there for 'you'.

A significant checkpoint in marriage revolves around **time** well spent together. The _quality_ of time spent with each other should always out-weigh the _quantity_ of time spent together. It is essentially [vitally/exceptionally] important that you find the time to romance your husband. Once again, romance

Searching Our Souls

is merely affectionate love, that we as humans, need to give more of - to each other and should be a keepsake in the marriage. Continuing to express your love through emotion is crucial to your marriage. Many men, as well as women, may feel romance is only an illusion that is too often fantasized as 'idealized love' and is not reality. Everything, whether it is material (as being tangible) or a strong belief in something (whether you are able to see it or not), originated with a thought. Anything that happens (although you may not be able to see it) and/or any thing of which consumes space (that which is visible to the natural eye), in/or of this world, was established based on theory. Either of those becomes very much 'real' to the beholder. (The wind blows and you cannot hold it in your hand nor are you able to see it, but it is definitely real.) Romance should be as much of an existence/fact to the individual as anything else. Therefore, romance is not an illusion/falseness. Romance declares passion, which unveils the desire to be with your husband. Romancing is a form of declaration/affirmation of your 'affectionate love' for your spouse. Continuing with the belief that romance is not a reality will erase love and keep love lacking in the relationship. Why do you think so many marriages "end up on the rocks", so to speak? Women and men, too often, allow unimportant things and/or people to intrude [disrupt] their ability to discern what is 'real' in their lives and what is not. If you feel you do not need romance in your life with your husband, you are wrong. How can you possibly discredit something which was a captivating force in your life guiding you to that special someone (your husband) initially? Romance was a part of the course of action displayed in dating your husband. This is part of the reason which encouraged you to become one. Allow romance to take on a new meaning in your marriage. If you have not considered romance to have credible worthiness in your marriage, change your way of thinking. Call it what you want, as long as you see it as a literary form of expressing your

Searching Our Souls

'affectionate love' for your husband. Remain faithful to your husband, whom should be the recipient of your loyalty. Do not leave romance out of your marriage because this will only make room for infidelity [adultery]. Get back on track - if you have fallen off - and become the person, you once were, towards your husband. (That person still resides within you. All you will have to do is re-introduce her to your husband.)

It is important to let your husband know that he is still desirable to you. You should expect the same affirmation from your husband. The feelings of closeness [togetherness] that you shared in the early stages of your dating and/or through the early years of your marriage should not cease. This closeness established passion between the two of you. **Don't let the 'passion' die!** Make time to spend romantic evenings together as often as possible. Allow yourself to become excited with anticipation. Reminisce on the good times you once shared and bring them back into your life to recapture the feelings. Enjoy each other! Continuously work on your togetherness [warm fellowship], as it is very crucial to your marriage.

If your work schedules do not permit you to spend as much time as you would like together, make a date with your spouse and be sure to make the time your relationship needs for survival. Do not allow your work/job to keep you separated from your loved one. This can happen very easily. Beware! Often different occupations create different life styles, although you are living together. You can find yourself in a position of loneliness, whereas intimacy in your marriage seems to have become a 'happening' of the past. Don't allow this to happen. You both should fight (struggle for equal time/show persistence) for the same level of intimacy in your marriage. You should make this a priority. There is no doubt that your employment is important because your employment provides income to support your financial obligations; however, don't give your life to your employer and neglect your

Searching Our Souls

spouse/child/children. This is truly a misplaced priority. Re-assess your priorities. Try working smarter and not longer! No ones employment should become more important than their spouse/child/children. Haven't you heard, "All work and no play leads to a very dull day?" **Well, it can also lead you into <u>divorce court</u>.** Learn how to balance your life between your 'job' and your 'marriage'. Conserve your energy and mind to create unforgettable moments in your marriage: moments to reflect on in years to come - when your employer is no longer a part of your life.

<u>Create playful moments together.</u> It is important for couples to have a common play ground. Allow yourself to develop interest and knowledge in your partner's fun interest or hobbies. You don't have to give up 'fun things' in life because you decided to marry. I am not saying you need to spend every moment together but try to spend as much time as you can doing things that will bring happiness to <u>both of you</u>. Sharing this type of quality time helps

you <u>stay together</u>. (I like to refer to it as the glue/cement that is needed to bond or repair cracks in the marriage.)

If one of you is constantly on the go doing things with someone else (such as a friend), your better half (spouse) as well as your marriage is being neglected. This is not good! Off-site marriage does not work. Occasionally suggest something in fun for the two of you to do. Allow your husband to suggest the same. Couples often create their own problems when it comes to determining what would be a mutual interest to share. The ladies will usually go about their own way doing 'their thing' and the men do the same. When one of you seems to be spending too much time with your own gender, questions usually surface such as: "Why don't we ever go out and do things together?" The most common answer to this question would be: "because you are always saying "Yes" to your friends." You have the power to change this. Try saying "YES" to your spouse more often and definitely as quickly as you would possibly say "YES" to your friends. When friends come around and make suggestions of fun things to do, how readily accepting are you? Give this immeasurable thought and try doing the same for your 'husband' as well as your 'friends'.

Speaking of *friends.* *Friends* are good to have around - providing they are really your true *friends*. Unfortunately, we are not always aware of the falsehood in our pretending *friends* until something happens to prove to us otherwise. **Good *friends* are rare**. Don't allow your door to swing open for others (such as your **so-called *friends***) on a regular basis, robing you of 'quality time' that you should spend with each other. After all, your home is your space on this planet that you have created together. People, so often, do not know when their 'welcome' has expired. So, stay in control of your domain (home) for the sake of peace and happiness in your marriage. Unfortunately, people can possess jealousy and will impose friction in your marriage, especially if you have a good one. **(Jealousy mainly suggests**

insecurities within ones self.) Take note of *friends* who may be 'single' and are tiring from their ***search*** of someone to share their lives with. Their insecurity may not be always obvious to you, but believe me, they would not mind having what you have - A husband! Your *friends* can be married also but should their marriage be in trouble, they would love to see yours in the same shape, if not worse. With marriage requiring such diligent [constant] work to keep blissful, who has the time to <u>sit</u> among others on a continuous basis? (If you have so-called *friends*, who never seem to have anything more important to do with their lives other than sit around you – beware of this awkward picture.) It's fine to share time with your *friends*, just be aware of the quantity of time you are spending with them. Always remain hopeful that your '*friends*' are really what they say they are – **'YOUR *FRIENDS*'. Better yet, try being a '*friend*' to your husband.**

Love each other and spend quality time together in your marriage. Again, this is not saying that you

Searching Our Souls

need to spend every moment together. You should also give each other space. Take a little time out for yourself. Absence <u>does</u> make the heart grow fonder. (I'm sure you've heard this before.) <u>It is a fact.</u> Allow yourself time to be missed. Everyone needs a personal [individual] outlet. This means you may have a hobby that is not of interest to your spouse and therefore, it requires you to be separated for awhile. That is fine. There is nothing wrong with this. Actually, it is healthy to have a hobby. Having a hobby allows you to escape from it all - from time to time - while freeing your stress. Now, you do not want to send a message to your mate that says, "you do not want to be bothered with them". This only means - we all need that 'special space' in our lives. This is also important for growth. This helps the individual stay in touch with one's <u>own</u> self. Our space allows us to take time out and regroup. Giving this space to each other tells your spouse you 'respect' their needs and at the same time it is a way of saying you 'love' and 'trust' them. Therefore, when you re-unite, you will be happy to be with one another again and quality time will take place. You and your spouse should try to remember the *quantity* of time spent is important, therefore let it be *quality* time that you share.

Modify your ways of doing things to spend quality time so that your marriage does not suffer. Plan some of your interest together to create the 'common playground' that your marriage needs and deserves - especially if you find that you are spending too much time apart. Respectfully give of your self to your friends but not more than you should give to your spouse.

Contrary to popular belief, marriages can and do work with fully committed individuals who are willing and able to do what it takes to build equity in their marriage and in their lives. It is not unrealistic that you should have certain expectations of your mate. However, never place expectations on someone if you cannot full-fill the same expectations for them. (Do not expect someone to do or give something to you that you are not capable of doing or giving yourself.) If you are not giving your loved one priority in your life, do not expect to be a priority in their life. Understand, what you give is what you will receive. In essence, when you are not giving anything, don't expect anything in return. It's just that simple.

Your marriage is to be looked upon as an ***investment***. Thereby, the both of you should be making contributions in that investment since marriage is a joint venture. In addition to time, you are *investing* your love to each other, which provides a strong foundation to build on. Your *investments in your marriage* are the same as any other investments you make, but in your marriage, they are of greater importance. Your investments should be protected in order to receive a good return. Any investor knows that his return from his investment should be more than what he has invested or at least equal to his investment. No one wants to take a loss in anything. Read on to learn how to protect your *investments in your marriage*!

When *investing* love, you immediately begin to establish an account through your heart as well as your loved one's heart, which should build an equitable [fair and just] return. (Meaning the same love you are giving should be returned to you.) This account is very similar to that of any investment account. As your love continues to grow, your sound investments should include - honesty, tenderness, compassion, sympathy, empathy, trust, understanding, etc. Through displaying your love, these traits become investments that are stored in your mate's/spouse's heart. For all of the above traits/elements are deposits that you <u>should</u> be making. When troubles arise and those deposits are not handled with care, you stand the risk of losing them when you 'say' and possibly 'do' the wrong things. Well, when this happens the person that your anger or hurt is directed towards, feels the loss of one (if not more) of those traits/elements previously given (deposited) which they have stored in their account (their heart). You, thereby, withdraw (take back) the things your have given (deposited) to establish that account. When this cycle is repeated, your account can become depleted (emptied/used up), leaving you with 'zero' (nothing). The base line here is clear. Be careful only by being considerate of someone else's feelings. If you don't mean positive things you express, don't say them. The same applies, **more so,** <u>to the negative</u>. After all, the 'negative' can cost you all that you have 'positively' invested. Protect your investments by treating your spouse and child, or children, the way you wish to be treated.

Learn how to use a more subtle approach, if you have not done so in your past. Use more of a meek and subtle approach to have your needs met while reserving and protecting your investments in your loved one(s) - as well as

yourself. You very well could get what you want- as well as what you need. In many cases you will find it is better just to think and not re-act.

Remember self-control!

RESERVED FOR SPECIAL NOTES:

In view of your marriage, what is the take on your position as a 'wife'? Evaluate yourself. What are you lacking in your marriage, if anything at all? What are some ideas you may have to support ways or changes to fulfill your lacking? (This is your call – so don't hold back.)

_____
_____
_____
_____
_____
_____
_____
_____
_____
_____
_____
_____
_____

Chapter Four

'PARENTHOOD'

Self-control, as best described, is the ability to exercise your 'will' preventing yourself from expressing strong emotion or acting impulsively. First and foremost, when you are in a relationship with someone whom you are not considering becoming married to, self-control needs to be applied. There are by far, too many women who take great advantage of the 'pleasures' that accompany making babies and fail to protect themselves from *becoming* '*Mothers*' when they are not yet ready to take-on the responsibility as a '*Mother*'. Where should responsibility lie? When you are an active participant the responsibility lies with **YOU first and foremost.** Be responsible to **protect yourself.** If you are not ready to become a Mother, take responsibility one step further to make sure your partner is protected <u>also</u>. **It can not get any more simplified than this!**

If and when you choose to become sexually active with someone, understand the proven possibilities and risk factors involved in unprotected sex. The consequences of engaging in unprotected sex, does not only promote the possibility of STD's [sexually transmitted diseases], but 'reproduction' becomes very possible. It is not fair to bring an unwanted child into this world especially when you are not a matured [responsible] adult to care for one. **This is wrong and there is no other way to put it.** If you have not matured enough to care for yourself (one way is being responsible to use protection), how can you possibly care for a child? If you feel you have matured enough to handle the responsibilities of caring for a child, you are then able to make a conscious decision to *become a 'Mother'*. **Until then, protect yourself!**

When you make the decision to bring a child into this world, upon that child's birth, you become a

'*Mother*'. To have a little person developing inside of you, whose life is totally dependent upon everything you do, is the 'greatest' of all miracles and a tremendous responsibility. The proper care you give to yourself during pregnancy, which nurtures your unborn, should not diminish after giving birth. It is most important that you understand the same person, who needed you during your pregnancy, <u>needs you more</u> at birth through adulthood. You, as the *Mother*, must realize you are choosing to be responsible for another human being until that human being can become responsible for himself. (Usually, this responsibility extends up to eighteen (18) years of a child's life and often longer.) This is a major responsibility for you as the 'parent'. There is much involved in being a 'good' parent and it is not an easy task. There are many books written on 'how to care for children' although none of them come with the birth of <u>your baby</u> to guide you through the years. Children are individuals, the same as adults. Just as differences

Searching Our Souls

exist in adults, so do they in children. You must realize children are only **little people**. They have feelings just as you and are very intelligent, even at an early stage of life. Respect them and the respect you give will be returned to you. (Here again, you are making an investment in your life.) Become a good example for your child. You are the most influential [important/significant] person your child has in his life. Your child's eye will be upon you although you may not consciously be aware of it. Always remember this! The examples you display will create an <u>everlasting vision</u> of **YOU,** in your child's mind. Always remain mindful of the image you could be projecting to your child. Again, you are the most 'powerful influence' that your child has.

As your child grows, you should administer *discipline* as well as *guidance*. As these two actions go hand-in-hand, they should be delivered through *patience*. Patience enables endurance [helps you to maintain your composure] when faced with the need to discipline your child/children. A child needs both, discipline and guidance, in order to become a productive citizen in later years. <u>*Guidance*</u> is direction, advice, and leadership. <u>*Discipline*</u> is the training and instruction of their minds and character in obedience to your rules and/or guidelines. *Discipline* is important because without it, your child will not be obedient to accept the guidance that you give. Both elements demonstrate Love and Caring to your child/children. You should not forfeit either through the up bringing of your child/children. *Discipline* and *Guidance* also forms respect. Respect should always remain throughout the years of one's life. The major benefit that comes with teaching your child to remain respectful will establish 'notability' [worthiness/value] in his adult life and that respect will be returned to him. For without *discipline* and *guidance,* a child will be lost in this world aimlessly wandering, forever. In raising your child teach him well and that, which you teach him, will never depart from him.

Searching Our Souls

If you don't know how to be a good parent, find out through reading or consult with someone who has a child that is practicing to be a 'good parent'. For starters, give him **LOVE** and have **PATIENCE**. A child should never be left to bring up himself. He/she constantly needs to know that you care. Taking the time to teach him **morals** [integrity, honesty, standards, principles] and **values** [worthiness, importance, qualities] in life will let him know that you care and love him. **Your child depends on you, as the parent, for his life.** Take time out to learn how to become a 'good parent' if you don't know how. Your child/children will surely be the affirmation of your teachings as time goes on. Position yourself to take note of their developing character and this will provide a signal to you as to the kind/type of parent you are to your child. If your child is out of control, it is probable because you allow him to be out of control, unless there is another explanation for his behavior: such as a health disorder. Parenting is a job that will never end until you, as the parent, leave this earth. Until that day comes, **LOVE** your child/children and follow through with the discipline and guidance you <u>must</u> administer to them and by all means, administer them with **PATIENCE**.

An abundance of parents, of today's world, have failed their children. Although your child is growing older, this does not mean you can surrender your position as 'the Parent'. Simply because your child is becoming self-assured does not mean to abandon the *'principles of parenting'*. Your child/children will always have needs for you – the parent - regardless of their age. This has become a major problem with our 'youth' today. Too many parents have forgotten the child and become so very "self-serving". Some have allowed <u>monetary</u> and <u>material</u> gifts to take control over their capacity (competence) as a 'parent', enabling their failure to set priorities in their lives, which have taught their child/children the wrong forms of authentic values. As a result, money and material items have become viewed as being of

Searching Our Souls

'greater' importance. Parents have also allowed themselves to be intimidated by believing there are alternatives in sparing 'guidance' and 'discipline'. There will be one definite alternative derived from this <u>lack of parenting</u> and that is '**No Respect**' for themselves or towards you, as the parent. When a child is allowed to not demonstrate respect to his parents, he feels free to disrespect others. **<u>This is wrong</u>. GOD** instructs us (as a people) to honor [respect] our Mothers and Fathers. **(There are no exceptions.)** Your child should be taught to respect 'you' as well as 'others'.

I have witnessed many parents bargaining with their child/children to show better behavior or to simply be obedient. This makes no sense and is utterly ridiculous. You are the 'parent' and when you are behaving as one, things of this nature would never take place. **Teaching your child starts at home and those lessons that are taught continue elsewhere**. Your child should have no doubt of your being the adult, "the parent", and what you teach your child will surely be displayed. You should not supply undeserved wants to your child in exchange for obedience. Being a 'YES' parent can do <u>harm</u> instead of <u>good</u> to your child. To say 'NO' to your child teaches him that he can not always have his way. Your child needs to become familiar with the word 'NO'. This is 'tough love'. **(The love you are still yet rendering to your child, when you say NO!)** Your primary focus is to grant (reward) your child with his <u>needs</u> as **GOD** grants them to you. This course of action should be conveyed and clearly explained to your child. When this has been established, their wants can be provided assuming they are deserving of them. When *'principles of parenting'* are learned and applied, your child/children will begin to establish morals and values in his/her life. As long as you up-hold your 'parenting rights', you will not lose your child to the world [streets]: and this will surely happen if you do not stand firm, in your own domain, to give 'guidance' with <u>love</u> and 'discipline' with <u>patience</u> to your child.

Our children, without a doubt, will become our future. Bearing this fact in mind, stop to do your '***soul searching***' and ask yourself this question, "What will my future hold for me?" If your child is not obedient unto you and continues to stray from the direction in which <u>you should be</u> providing, that question is very hard to constructively answer. When given considerable thought to that question, it really becomes scary because so many of us in our 'golden years' will be in deep trouble if we continue to overlook our children's needs and cannot be firmer - primarily in the discipline and guidance of them. Our children must understand how to be in acceptance of our guidance and discipline of which is administered to them. Therefore, it is vitally important to perform your job well as a 'parent' giving direction to your child. Unless, you teach your child morals and values in life, he/she will have nothing to offer to this world and as a result, will not receive what he/she should be deserving of. **Many children stand in need of constant assurance of their parent's 'caring' and 'love'.** We fail our child/children when we make choices, on numerous occasions, to go about our way doing some things that does not include them. [One main example of this: to leave your child behind in the care of someone else (with some women, it does not matter who the person is) as long as you are able to do as you please. Or worse: to leave your child alone to fend for himself.] Our children's lives are important and they are in preparation of becoming 'adults'. You should never lose sight of this because if your actions spell 'I don't care' - so will theirs, as they grow into 'adulthood'.

Take some time to pause and consider the following:

- Will your child be there caring and continuing to give you love or will your child become lost and remain to be lost in

this world never knowing the true meaning of love?
- Or, could your child grow into being an 'adult' never knowing if you genuinely cared and loved him?
- Will your child possibly grow up and forget about you altogether?

These are serious questions that much thought [consideration] should be given towards. Are you able to provide positive answers to any or all of those questions? What would your answers be? To help provide positive answers to any of those questions there are principles provided to aid you in your job as a 'parent'. **These *principles* are written in the Bible. GOD** tells us to – **{Train up a child in the way he should go; and when he is old, he will not depart from it. (Proverbs 22:6)} GOD** also gives you further instruction on raising your child such as: {**Foolishness is bound in the heart of a child; but the rod of correction shall drive it far** from him. (Proverbs 22:15)} Other instructions provided states: **{Apply thine heart unto instruction, and thine ears to the words of knowledge. Withhold not correction from the child. (Proverbs 23:13)}** Pass that knowledge on to your children so they may grow into adulthood assuming complete responsibility to live according to **God's** instructions and pass the same on to their children - and so on. This is the <u>most rewarding investment</u> you can make that <u>will</u> <u>deliver</u> a **<u>guaranteed</u>, <u>valuable</u> <u>return</u>**. Create an investment account through your child/children. Our children will most surely become our future one-day! **That you can – take to the bank!**

A Mother should remain 'A MOTHER' on all occasions. I say this again because too many parents use a '***Buddy System***' when dealing with their child/children. Your child needs you as a 'Parent' and not a '*Buddy*'. When you are too complaisant [obliging, ready to do what will please] and /or carefree [not being watchful or providing serious attention] you are losing your 'power' and 'rank' [position] that should reign over your child/children. As a result, respect will soon become absent. Trying to be your child's *'buddy'* will only rob you of the love and respect of which you should be giving and receiving as the 'parent'. **The *'Buddy System'* does not work.** Your child/children will have buddies and/or friends to come and go throughout his/her life. On the other hand, you will **always** be the 'parent'. Do not forfeit [give-up] that rank [position] for any reason or to anyone. Stand proud to be 'the parent' in your child's life and be a good one. Being a good parent automatically makes you a 'friend' in your child's eyes. Allow your child only to see you as a 'friend' and continue being that 'friend' by maintaining to be a 'good parent' always to your child/children.

A Mother and Father *should provide support* for their child/children - not only financially - but also emotionally, spiritually and physically. There are fathers who do not acknowledge this. It seems as though many men feel that their contribution in their child's life has been full-filled as long as they provide income (dollars and cents). This is far from the truth. <u>A child needs more</u>. A child does not know the value of a dollar until he is of the age to earn his own. Your child's Father should give of himself (time) to your child and not just dollars and cents - and you, as the mother, should always remain focused to see that your child/children receives much more. Your child's Father, as well as yourself, should spend quality time with your child doing things to create a history of love and understanding. Children grow so rapidly and become adults in what seems a short while. Through out your child's life, show love and cherish the time granted to you. Enjoy and share in your child's activities. Participate in playful moments together. This also gives you the opportunity to be a 'child at heart' again, yourself. You should never be too adult to enjoy your child/children. Through your enjoyment of time shared, you are creating moments that your child will never forget. Your child will always remember good times shared and past them on to their young - some day. This is how legacies are made. You will continue to live forever in your child's heart and your contributions to his happiness will be passed on to his child. How Wonderful! It is well worth your being a good Mother, in all ways possible to your child, while making sure your child/children's father contributes the same. It has often been said, " It takes a Village to Raise A Child". If it takes a village to raise a child, it definitely takes a 'Mother' and a 'Father'. There are so many 'single parents' today and it is basically due to the fact of people not assuming responsibility for their actions. They are irresponsible people engaging in sexual relations for the wrong reasons and do not stop to consider the consequences that could result from their actions. Again, the consequences of unprotected sex does not only promote the possibility of sexually transmitted diseases (STDs), **reproduction becomes very possible**. Your child should be a product of 'love' and not <u>'lust'</u>. When you are not in 'love' with the man in your life and if you are using him for sexual pleasure, producing unwanted children, you are not only degrading yourself but you are also creating destruction.

Should you be unmarried, you should <u>never need</u> to seek any type of *support* from your child's father. A mature (responsible) adult male, **MAN**, should be too willing to extend help to the Mother of his child in providing care. Your child is a product of the father, as well as you - the mother. If he cared enough about you to impregnate you, then he should care enough about your child and give your child the support he/she needs.

Do not alter the love of your child to gain from your child's father. Do not use your child as a 'bargaining tool'. Men and women are guilty of this. Parents, the mother and the father, should try to remain on the same accord for the <u>welfare</u> [benefit/happiness] of the child. This means, if you cannot reconcile your differences to see a future together as man and wife, at least put forth the effort to build a good and decent relationship for the benefit of your child. If you are divorced from your child's father, <u>don't divorce your child</u>. Your status and capacity as a **mother** is completely different from that of being someone's spouse.

Children often bear a 'burden of guilt' when they have parents that were never married or parents who become divorced. Your child needs to understand that some people, for whatever reasons, cannot live together in matrimony. This is your job to clearly explain this to your child, thereby relieving your child of any guilt feelings of which could have been inadvertently (unintentionally) created by you. The child so often gets caught in the middle and this is very unfair to a child. When this happens, your child will suffer the loss. **<u>Don't make your child a victim of circumstance.</u> <u>Your child is not</u> <u>responsible for you; YOU ARE RESPONSIBLE FOR YOUR CHILD.</u>**

In essence, with love in your heart and *soul* along with wisdom through GOD's teachings, you will - by instinct - know the right things to do for and by your child. Love serves as a guide to give your child a meaningful life. This sometimes means - tough love. Never forget children grow up and do become adults.

DO YOUR VERY BEST FOR AND BY YOUR CHILD WITH LOVE AND UNDERSTANDING AND WHEN THAT CHILD BECOMES AN ADULT, HE/SHE WILL DO LIKEWISE UNTO YOU!

Searching Our Souls

RESERVED FOR SPECIAL NOTES:

In view of your role, as a 'parent', are you giving all of what you should be giving to your child? List the pros (the things which you do) and the cons (the things of which you don't do) of your interactions with your child/children and respectively prioritize them. Overall, how do you rate yourself as being a 'good parent – a Mother'?

(It is important that you be truthful to yourself.)

_____
_____
_____
_____
_____
_____
_____
_____
_____
_____

Brenda S. Williams

Chapter Five

'THE SPIRITUAL SIDE OF YOU'

<u>**The "Bible"**</u>- <u>the best book of many books ever to have been written</u> - provides to all a consecutive history of mankind beginning with the story of the 'creation of man'. **{In the beginning GOD created the heaven and the earth. (Genesis 1:1)}** Upon his refining heaven and earth, he then decided to create MAN. **{GOD created MAN in his own image. (Genesis 2:27)}**

You, as ***God's <u>miracle creation</u>***, are made of flesh and not stone. Within your flesh, there is a resting-place, referred to as your '***Soul***'. [The ***Soul***, being the immortal (everlasting) part of man.] When we engage [connect] in **'*Searching Our Souls*'** we can find peace, joy and happiness even in the midst of troubled times; providing we are living our lives based on **God's** instructions. To know this alone, should bring satisfaction to you immediately.

Everyone will be confronted with adversities [troubled-times] in their life, on occasion. If and when things are not going right for you in your life, have you ever asked yourself "why me"? Sure you have! Haven't we all, at one time or another. This question we sometimes pause to ask ourselves, makes us take complete inventory of all aspects [appearances/directions] resulting from the ways of which we have chosen to live our lives. **This is - "*Searching Our Souls*"** and it is a much-needed process, especially in today's world. We consult the spiritual side of our being that is deep within us (**our *soul***) for answers. This is where you will always find the 'right' answers you are seeking.

There is a <u>Spiritual Side</u> to everyone and when you are not yielding in your life to that spiritual side, you will continually struggle to find peace, joy, love and genuine happiness. For all of these qualities [assets] can not be bought nor sold and can be blessings to you just for the asking. These assets will manifest [become clear/evident] when you seek **GOD** and have complete recognition and trust in Him. After giving **God** complete acceptance [possession of your life], your blessings will unfold and begin to flow. As those blessings are acknowledged, by giving 'thanks' to **God**, (no matter how big or small) they will continue to come your way. Understand when I say, "**God** is in complete control of everything you 'say' and 'do' when you give your love and heart to him." There is nothing you do or say on your own without the graces of **God**. He is able to hear and see all. **{The eyes of the LORD are in every place, beholding the evil and the good. (PROVERBS 15:3)}** After all, you are his *miracle creation* and no one on this earth is capable of understanding you as he does.

GOD is *our* 'Heavenly Father'. **GOD** is greater than anyone existing in this world. He reigns over all humankind and all things. All men, women and children are children of **GOD**. Our main and primary focus should be to acknowledge him as '***Our Heavenly Father***'. Therefore, we must be obedient unto him to be worthy of his many blessings and claim our seats beside him. How 'great' those blessings are! It is sad that so many people are unmindful of their many blessings [riches] that **God** has given them. **God** unselfishly created human kind and placed in our possession treasures and powers. Yet we continue with our daily lives not hesitating to identify with the '*miracle creation*' that we are and never use the powers we possess as we take our treasures for granted.

So many people take their blessings for granted, not ever giving a second thought as to what or how life would be 'without' them. **God** created you to feel, hear, see, taste and smell. Remember your five senses? Oh well, you probably haven't stopped long enough to look upon these as 'gifts' and be 'thankful' to have them.

Searching Our Souls

Stop and take complete inventory of your blessings/riches and give considerable thought to the following:

1) Have you ever imagined what your life would be like if you could not reach out to touch and feel someone (or yourself for that matter)?

2) How would your life differ if you were blind and could not see?

3) How would your life differ if you were deaf and could not hear?

4) How would your life differ if you were mute and could not speak?

5) How would your life differ if you were crippled and could not walk or completely incapacitated [disabled]?

Another of our many blessings we so often take for granted is the ability to smell and taste.

6) How would your life be if you could not enjoy good food or drink because you were unable to smell or taste?
7) How would things change if you were unable to use your brain?
8) **Do you have all of your limbs for use? Are you able to use your arms and legs?**
9) View your body in its entirety - what if you were 'a human vegetable' and did not have the ability to do <u>anything</u> for yourself?
10) What do you think would happen if your 'heart', the central point of your being, stopped pumping blood through your arteries to all parts of your body?

These are, but a few, of your many 'riches'. If you haven't given consideration to any of these thoughts, may I suggest you do so? **You were created with vital organs, bones, muscles and nerves and referred to as a 'miracle'. You are a**

rare specimen. You have been given all the **wealth** to proclaim in this world. Count your blessings and give daily 'thanks' for them. Discontinue stating complaints about things that you don't have. You see - some are less fortunate than you are. Don't take any of your blessings for granted because you could find yourself in a situation that would deliver a very different 'way of life'. There should **not** be a day to begin nor reach its' end without <u>you</u> taking note of your many '**riches**' and '**giving thanks**' for all of them as <u>your</u> '**blessings**'. Never ignore the fact of your being a 'significant creation'. You have been provided the necessary tools to make a 'positive mark' in this world. **Utilize them wisely!**

A man's [woman's] *understanding* is limited to things of the earth. You will undoubtedly make mistakes [errors] because there are no 'perfect' humans residing on this earth. When you fail to yield to your spirit, you will unquestionably make a wrong decision [choice]. Once you reflect on the wrong choice you've made, all is not lost. Accept it! Learn from your <u>wrong</u> and strive to make it <u>right</u>. Allow your errors to rectify [correct/revise] your choices. The 'wise man' learns from his mistakes and does not continue to go through life repeating them. If you should mistakenly or deliberately hurt someone and realize your wrongdoing, ask for *'forgiveness'*. Yes! Humble yourself to ask them to 'forgive' you for hurting them and **<u>do</u> <u>not</u>** repeat the same 'wrong'. Speak-up to say, "I'm Sorry!" and ask for absolution. (Make certain that "I'm Sorry" is a sincere apology and not a reference to your character.) If **God** can forgive us all, then who are we - if we can not forgive one another?

Do not permit your *pride* [*self-importance*] to block your better judgment. *Pride* often gets in the way and destroys our opportunity to progress [advance]. For as long as you continue to live, you will never know all there is to know of this world about any particular one or any particular thing. When you remain detachable [constantly moving], refusing some sort of guidance, you are destined [doomed] to fail. Take the 'helping-hand' of guidance that is being given to you to assist you through your many endeavors [attempts/efforts] as you pursue your journey through life. Open the door to your heart so **GOD** can enter and guide you through this 'tunnel of life' that we all share. You see you are not in this world alone and cannot stand alone in it. You need **God's** strength and guidance to live a life of that which **God** has created for you.

God gave his son, ***JESUS CHRIST***, complete authority over everything and that includes us as human beings. Through **JESUS,** and only **JESUS,** are we then able to have sufficient power to govern the happenings in our daily lives. **JESUS** was sent to teach of our Heavenly Father's <u>Love</u> and <u>Understanding</u>. **JESUS** wanted earthlings to know that **God** is real to all of us and not just to him, as his son. Many did not believe in **God,** although **God** used **Jesus** to exhibit his powers as well as pass on the delight and complete wonderfulness of his compassion and love. As an end result, **JESUS** was crucified and paid for our debts. Thereby, saving all of us from sin. How is it possible for anyone <u>not</u> to believe in **God** or his son, **JESUS**, today? For it is because of **God's** son, **JESUS,** that we are existing in this world this very moment.

God has given all of us *laws*, <u>**Commandments**</u> **(Exodus: Chapter 20),** so that man, woman and child may live theirs lives to the fullest in the midst of this troubled world. These Commandments are set forth to give us direction *governing* our daily lives on earth and are meant to be his *expectations of WOMAN*. We, Men and Women, are to respect **God's** *laws* and be obedient to them.

Man will sometimes place demands on you that are much harder to full-fill, with no reward to gain. Yet somehow, man is who will be followed. Keeping this in mind should help you to do **God's** will with the greatest of ease. With man guiding you, you are only able to go as far as man takes you. With **God** as your leader, you can go as far as <u>you</u> want to go. That alone, in itself, is more than man is willing to allow. When you follow **God** as he instructs, your heart and *soul* will be connected - creating harmony - while renewing your mind [the thought process]. Your spirit will be connected to **God's** spirit guiding you, every day of your life, to do 'good will' unto others. You will know exactly what it means to love <u>unconditionally</u> and you will be able to <u>**'Thank God'**</u> at the end of the day for all of your blessings with joy in your heart and excitement to awake tomorrow facing a new day - filled with more blessings. It is such a relief to know that **God** promises us not to worry about tomorrow, for it <u>will</u> take care of itself. When you place **God** first in your life, all needs will be added unto you.

    God also tells us: **Ask and it shall be given you.**
    Seek and ye (you) shall find.
    Knock and it shall be opened unto you. (Matthew 7:7)

    How many men or women do you know to so graciously offer the same? This is only a sample of **God's** promises to all humankind. **God's** <u>ultimate</u>

promise is '**eternal life**'. With **Faith**, it all belongs to you and there are no exceptions based on who you are or may have been in the past. He has no prejudices. **{For there is no respect of persons with God. (Romans 2:11)}**

God is very compassionate and forgiving. If and when you should make a wrong decision, he will always be there to comfort you and see you through whatever you are dealing with. When you 'yield' to **God's** guidance, he will bless you with the insight /perception to carry on. This is discernment. You <u>need</u> discernment to help guide you on making the 'right' choices/decisions in your life. Discernment will also help you to see the 'error of your ways'. **God** will never abandon you. This is <u>only</u> <u>one</u> 'promise' of your *inheritance* that you will receive through exercising your <u>faith</u> in **GOD,** through his son, **JESUS CHRIST**. **GOD** will never abandon you. Have complete faith in his promises, for they are 'bona fide'.

Searching Our Souls

Through **Faith** [which is complete acceptance of a truth that cannot be clearly demonstrated or proved by the process of logical thought: in addition to being the substance of things hoped for [**mere believing**] and the evidence of things not seen], <u>only</u> are you able to receive **God's complete** promises. There are several levels of faith such as: strong faith, little faith, temporary faith, etc. Whatever level your faith is on, make certain that it is unfeigned [real, sincere, genuine] and not just mental [only in the mind]. Faith, more simply stated, is to **believe** in **God's** words and **do** them.

We so often go through life not knowing before hand where our paths will lead. When the path you take approaches a fork in the road, which way will you go? This is the question that will require an immediate answer for you to carry on. With **God** having first place in your life, acknowledging him as your **Heavenly Father**, a light will be placed at your feet to give you the guidance needed to pursue your journey as you '*search* your *soul*'. {**Trust in the**

LORD with all thine heart, and lean not unto thine own understanding. In all thy ways acknowledge him, and he shall direct thy paths. (Proverbs 3:5-6)}

God specializes in the things that may occasionally seem impossible to you. Allow him to share your life and you will find that **with God, 'all things are possible'**.

There are very few guarantees in this life but one is certain, and that is '**Death**'. Facing this truth, you have a choice. When you consider death as **'the inevitable'** [inescapable], consider how you are 'living' your life - <u>while you have it</u>. Only one person will live your life and that person is **YOU**. You have been provided all the necessary equipment to become whatever you desire in this life. With all power vested in you by our 'heavenly father' [our creator], you are enabled to have complete control over your destiny by choice. **{JESUS is the way, the truth and the life: no man cometh unto the Father, but by me. (John 14:6)}** Only through

JESUS, can we become empowered [have unleashed powers] to live as we choose and become prosperous in all areas of our daily living. Again, there is a formula we must live by in order to experience joy/happiness in life. That formula consists of placing **JESUS** first in your life, **O**thers second and **Y**ourself - last. The before letters of this formula signifies – **JOY**. Without **JESUS** in your life, serenity [peace] and happiness [tranquillity] will be unknown to you. Only through **JESUS,** can we remain saved to demonstrate our goodwill as **God's** children.

LEARN AND OBEY GOD'S *LAWS* [COMMANDMENTS]!

They are as follows: (EXODUS 20:3-17)

1) **Thou shalt have no other gods before me.**
2) **Thou shalt not make unto thee any graven image.**
3) **Thou shalt not take the name of the LORD thy God in vain.**

4) **Remember the sabbath day, to keep it holy.**
5) **Honour thy father and thy mother.**
6) **Thou shalt not kill.**
7) **Thou shalt not commit adultery.**
8) **Thou shalt not steal.**
9) **Thou shalt not bear false witness against thy neighbour.**
10) **Thou shalt not covet thy neighbour's house (nor anything that is thy neighbour's).**

JESUS set forth a **new commandment** on the day of his **'Last Supper'** with his apostles/disciples. **That commandment clearly states "To love one another". (John 13:34)**

Learn and master how to become the **'captain'** of your *'soul'* through constant *search* and have faith in **God** to believe in yourself. Upon exercising this type of *'soul searching'*, you will unveil [expose] an intuitive reliance [awareness of confidence/trust/faith within] that will nourish you into being a better individual. **JESUS** spoke words delivering the same message by saying, **"According to your faith - be it unto you". (Matthew 9:29)**

In summary, *"If you believe you can – You will"* and *"If you believe you cannot – You will not."*

Let us all continue *'Searching Our Souls'* to find the **LOVE** and **AMAZING GRACE** which we all have been blessed with to share among one another.

Only then, will we be able to continue on 'Earth' as it is in 'Heaven'.

GOD Bless!

RESERVED FOR SPECIAL NOTES:

Are you still, if you ever were, in doubt of how you are to live your life? Who have you chosen to be your leader – MAN or GOD? Have you dropped your pride and 'surrendered' yourself, so that you may have an everlasting life? Above all, have you accepted JESUS as your 'Lord and Savior' and acknowledged GOD as your 'Heavenly Father' with the understanding of Faith, which will erase all of your doubts and fears? Give yourself to JESUS and <u>he</u> will take <u>you</u> to our 'Father'!

About the Author

In addition to being a writer, Brenda Williams is a daughter, sister, aunt, great aunt, wife, mother, grandmother and a licensed master cosmetologist. Having shared all of these icons, in the most humanistic manner, has warranted her with substantiation to know that she has a great understanding of *love* and *respect* for humanity.

Through the years of her life, while maintaining her faith to believe in a higher power, has strengthened her being. Among the things she has learned in her life, the most important one is, to believe in your self and trust in God. For it is he, who will bless you to become the person you should be in this life.

Printed in the United States
777700001B